NATIONAL GEOGRAPHIC

It Can Fly

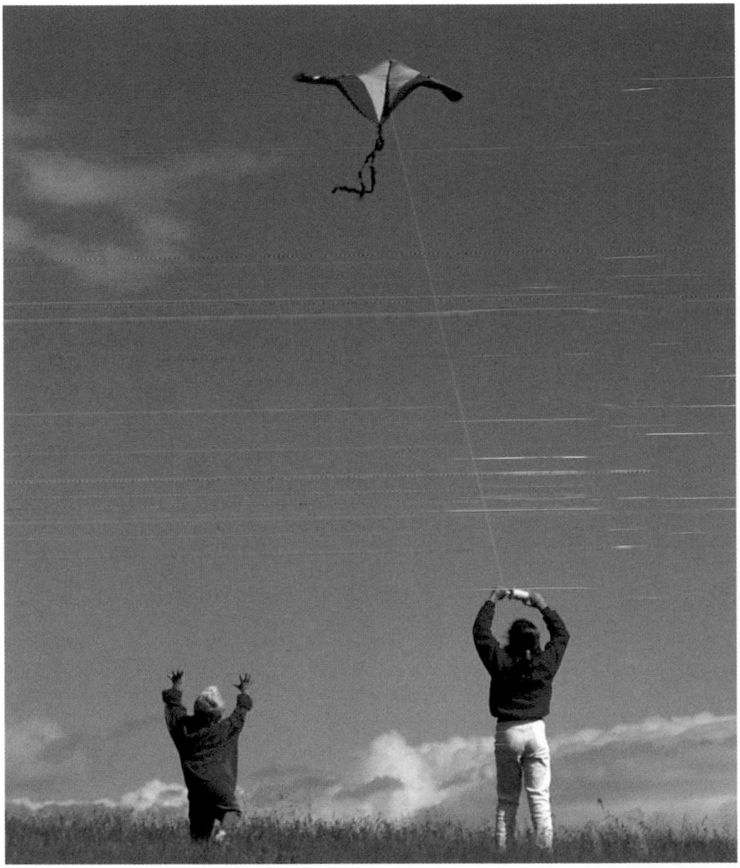

Kevin Biggs

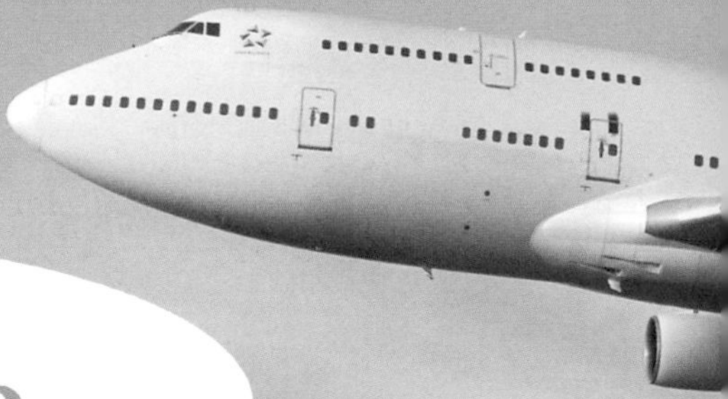

airplane

2

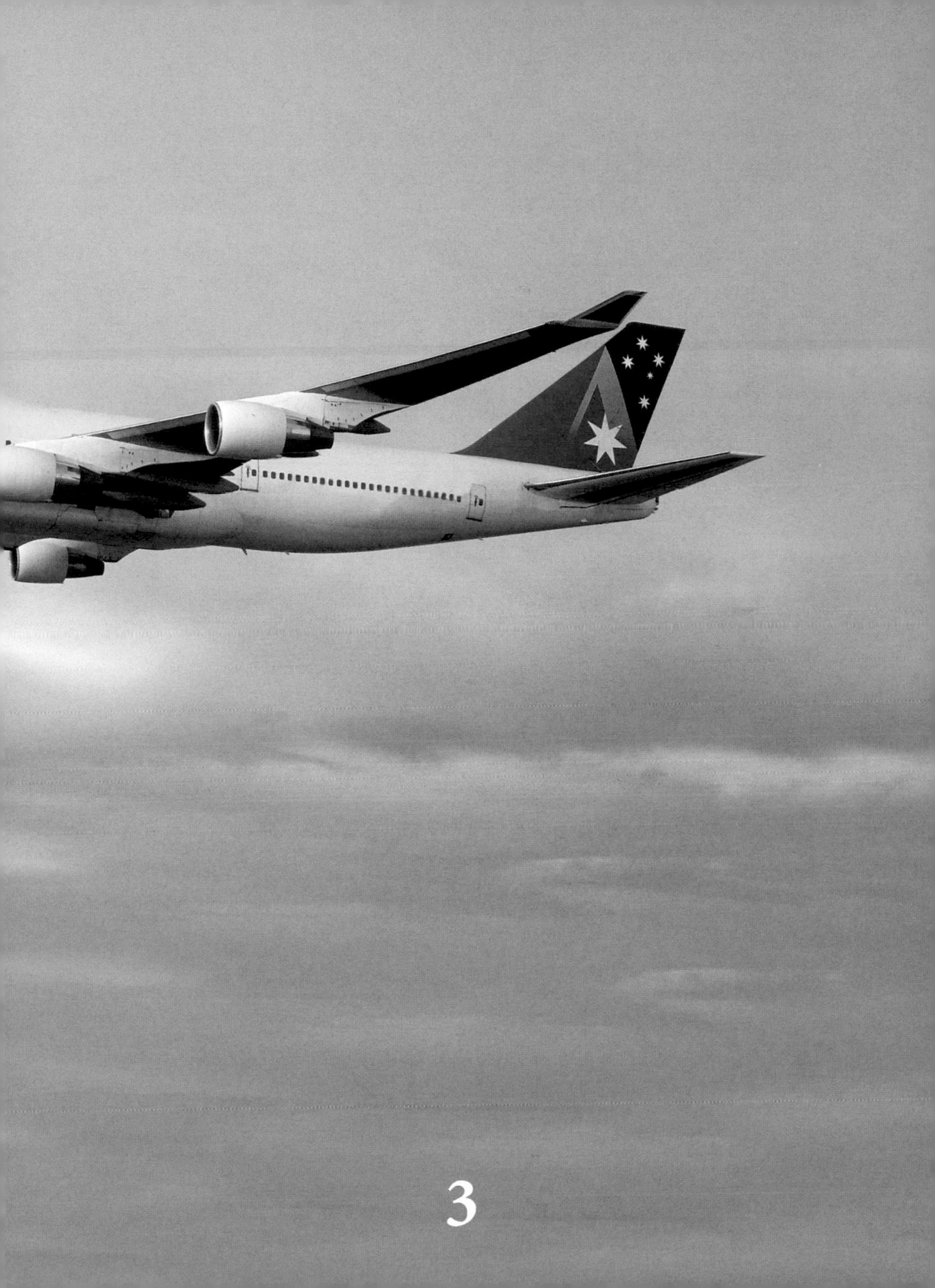

3

4

helicopter

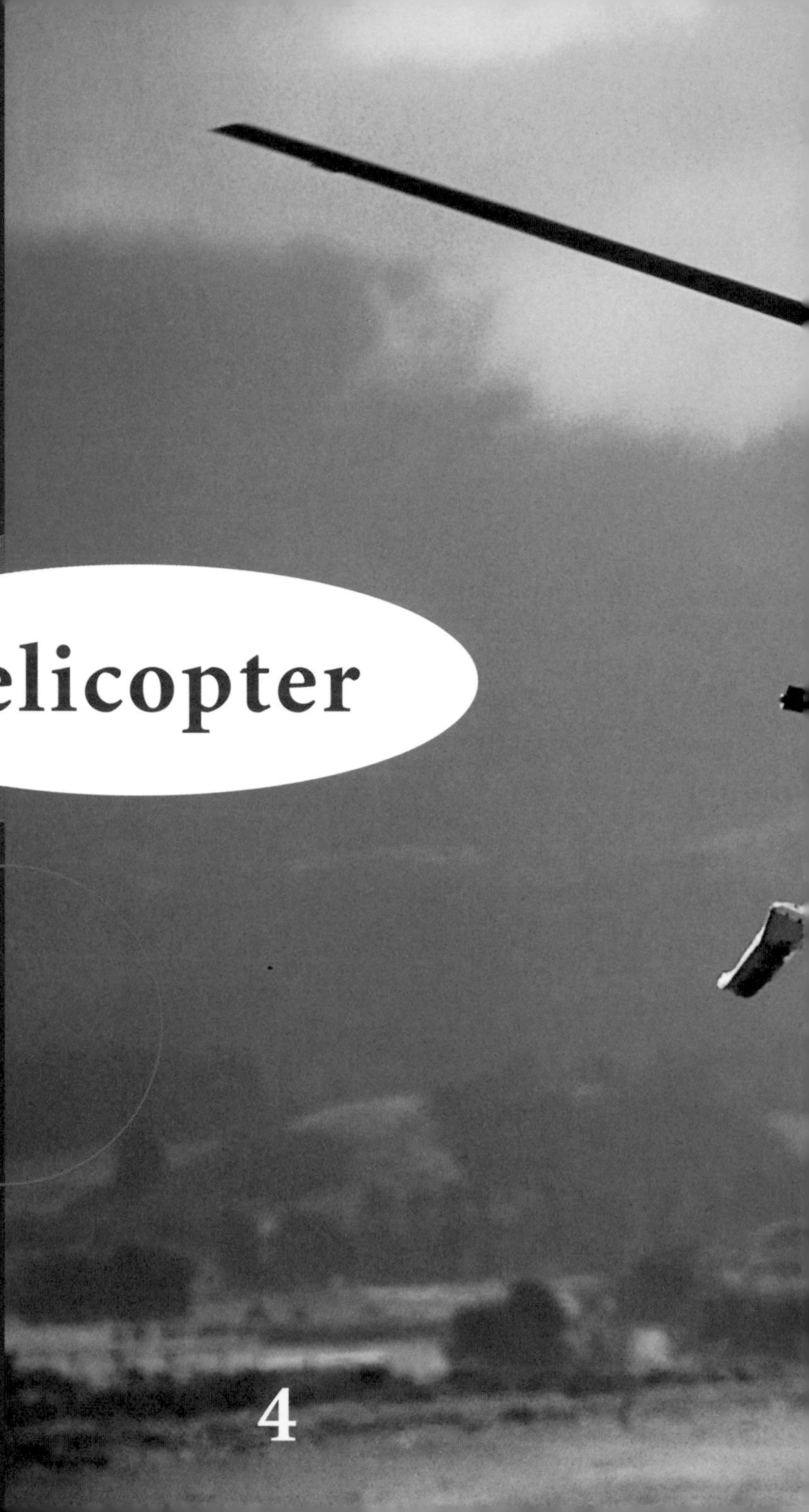

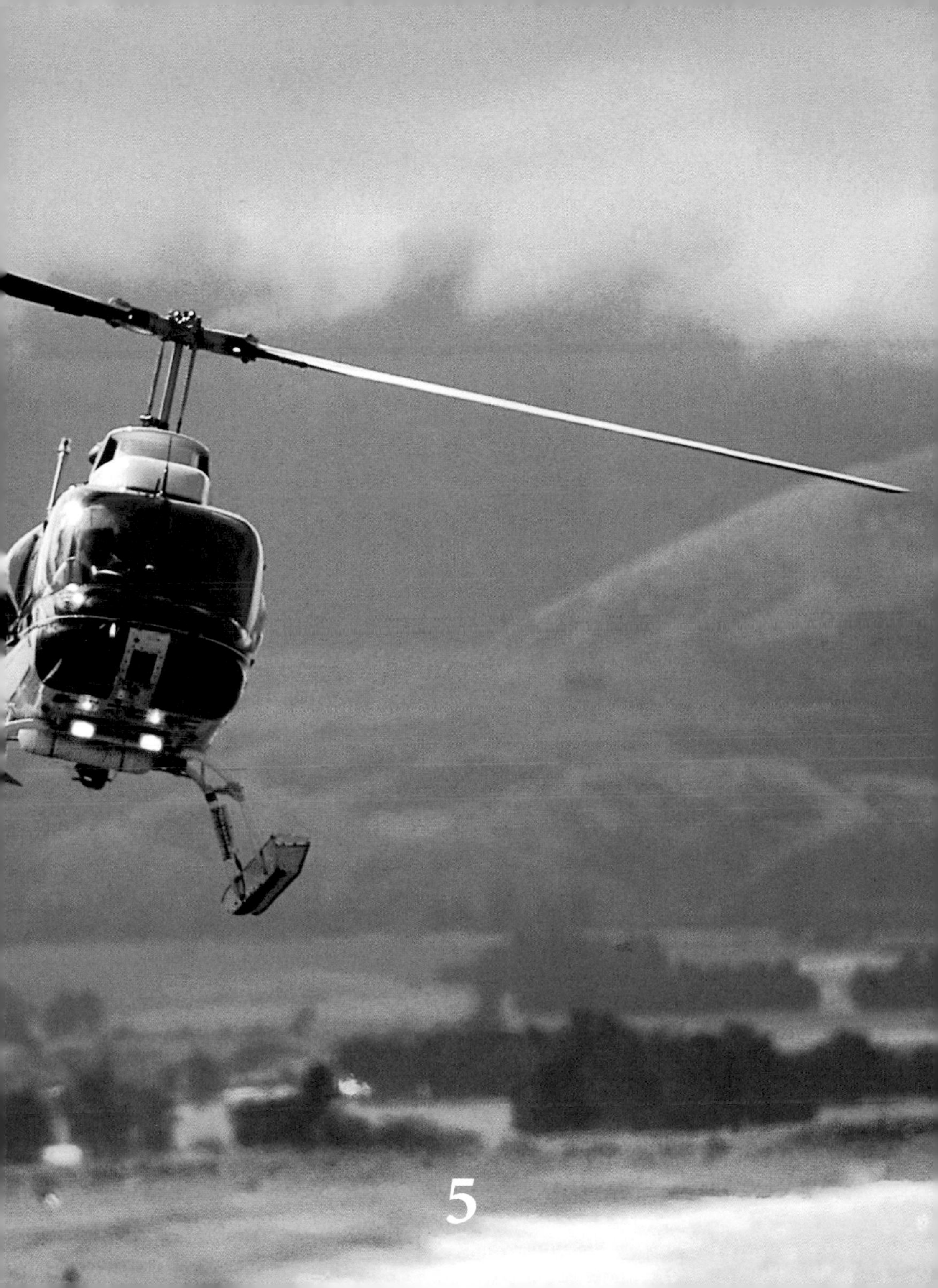

5

blimp

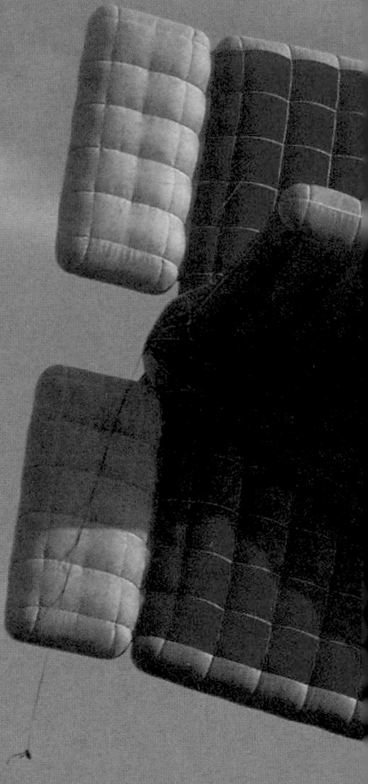

6

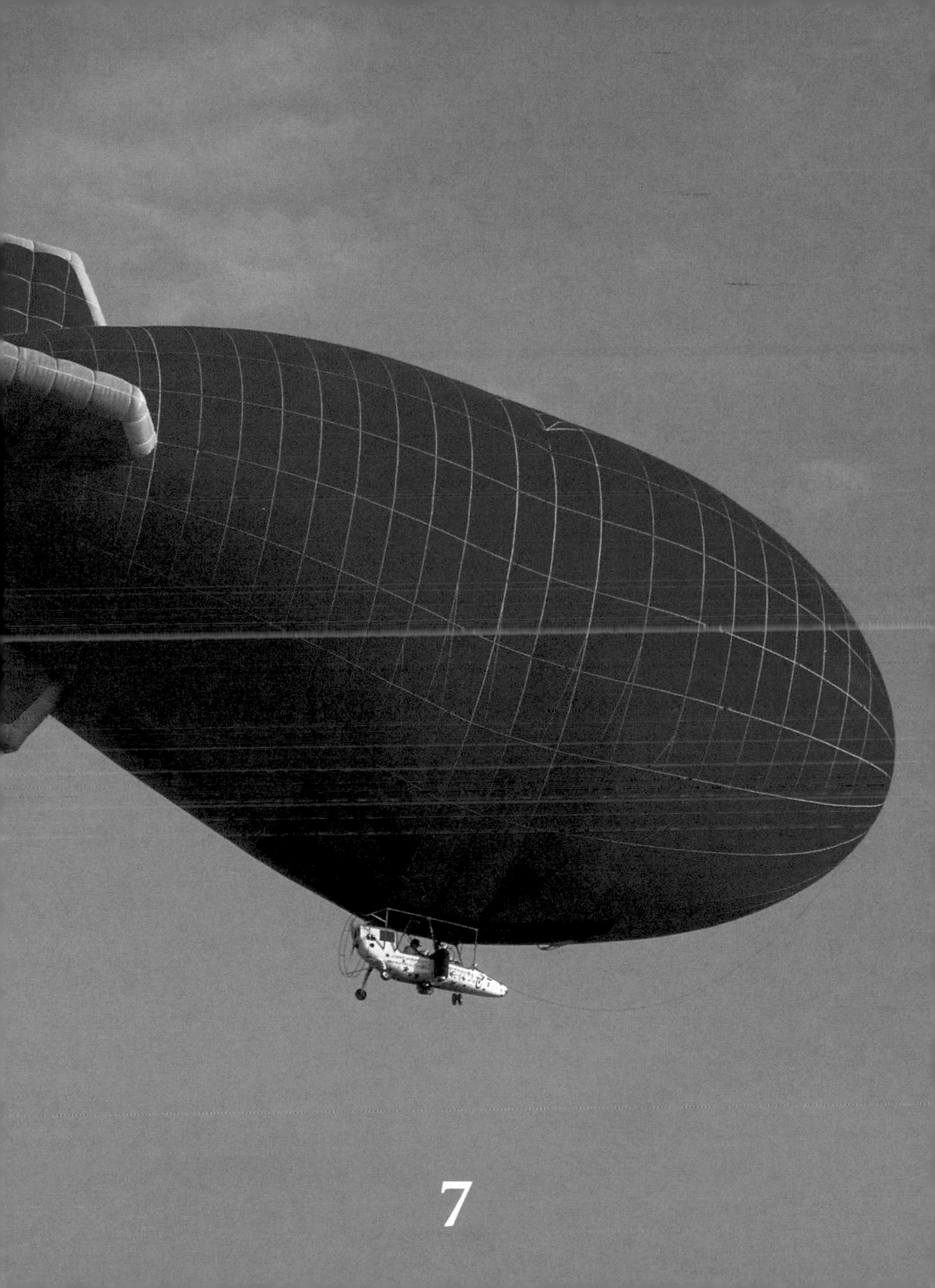

7

hot-air balloon

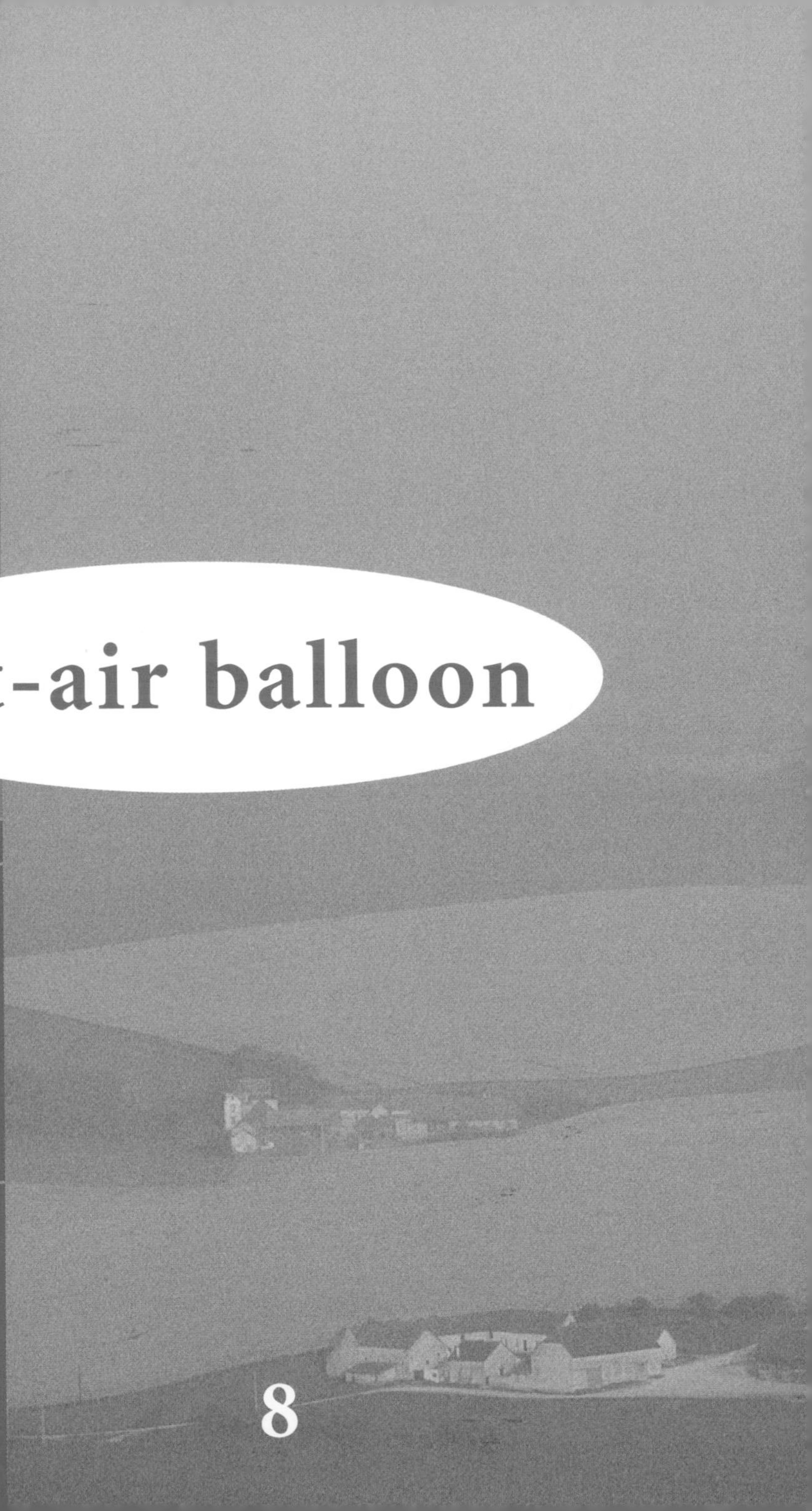

8

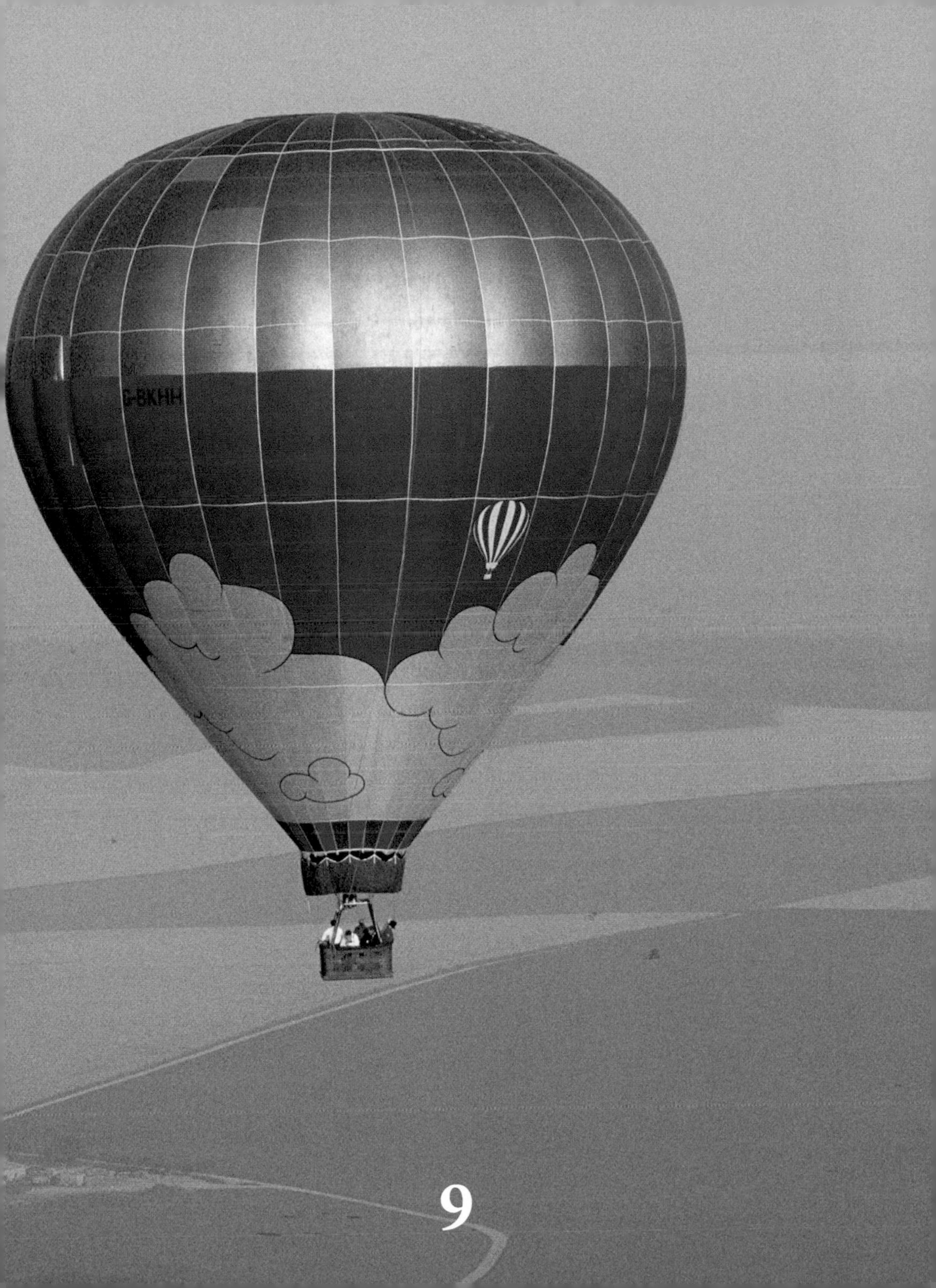

9

hang glider

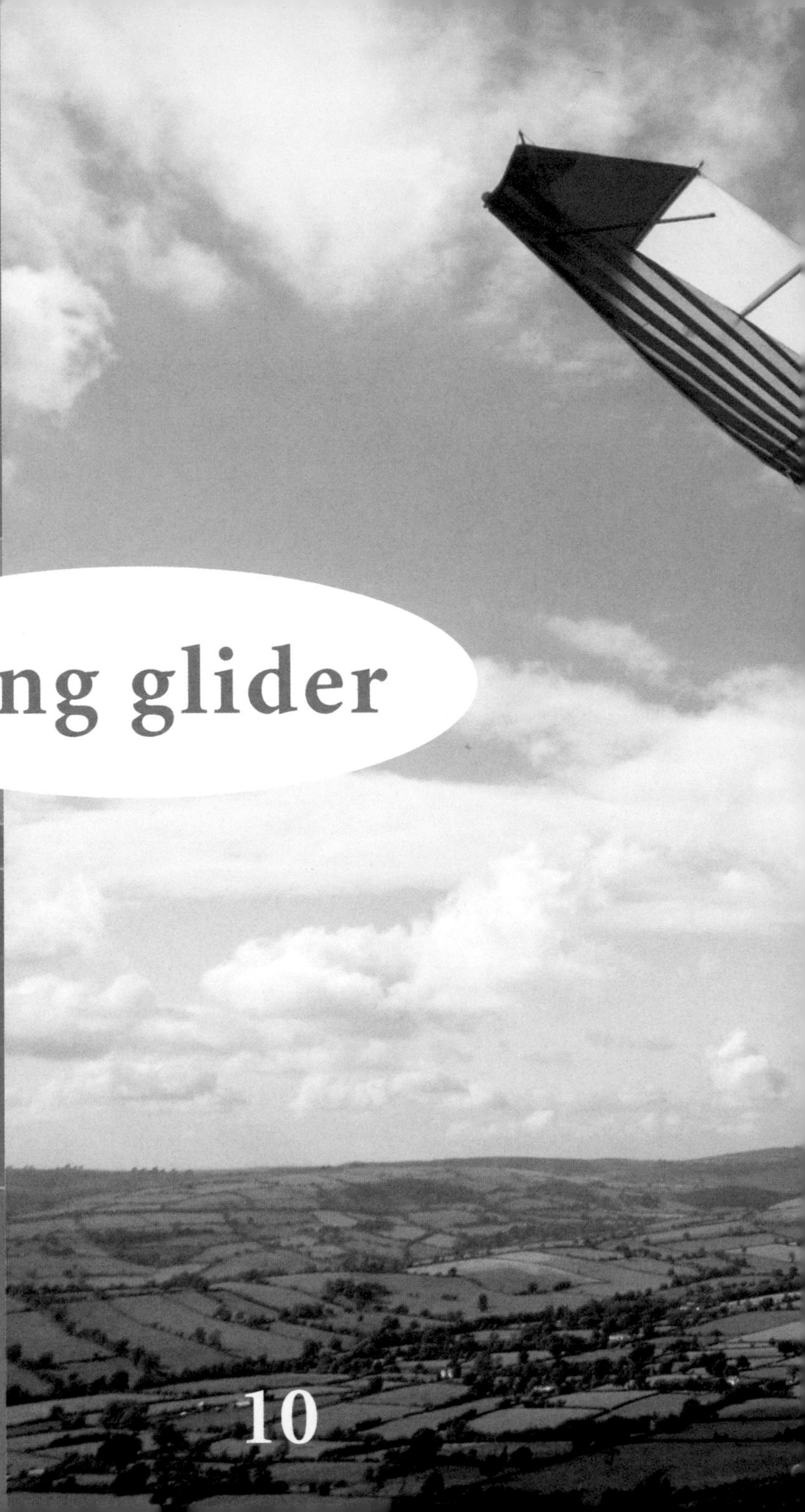

10

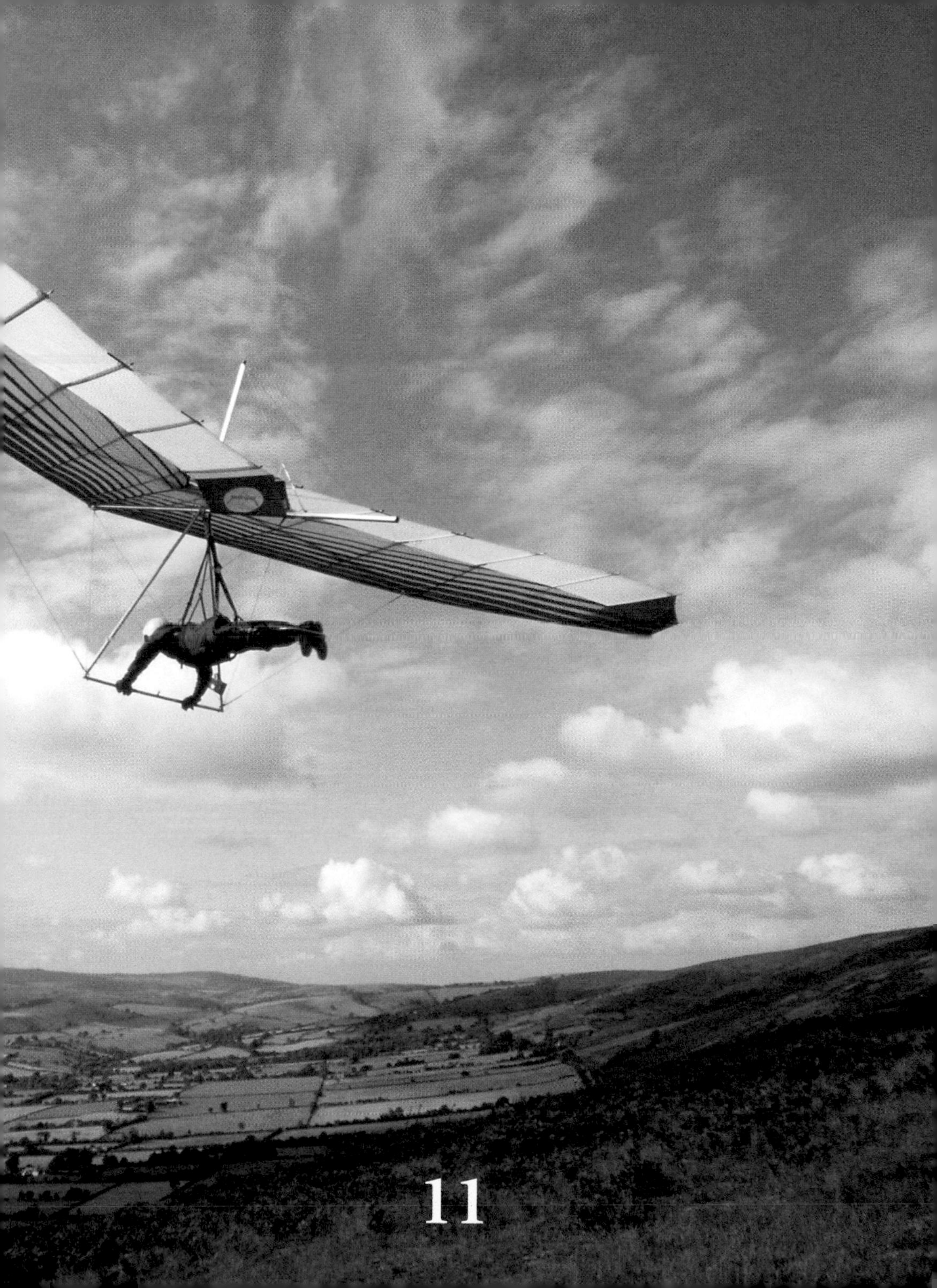

kite

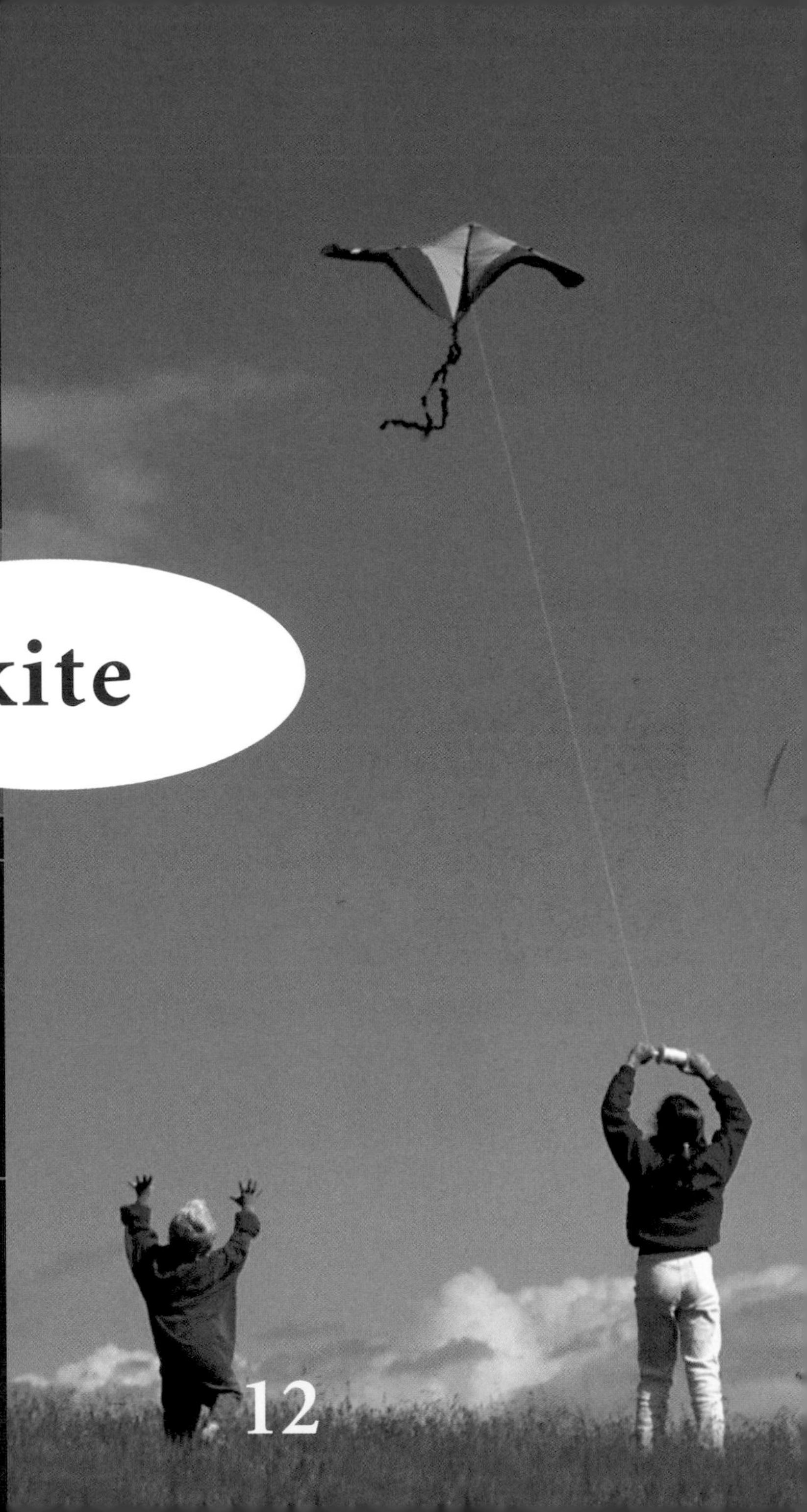